Nuggets of Encouragement

Living Each Day with Grace & Love

Dr. Rebekah McCloud

Nuggets of Encouragement: Living Each Day with Grace & Love
by Dr. Rebekah McCloud

Cover and Interior Design by Big Easy Creative
Front Cover Image licensed for use from Adobe.com

Order Direct
https://www.drrebekahmccloud.com

ISBN 978-0-9748179-9-6

Produced and Printed in the United States of America
10 9 8 7 6 5 4 3 2

The views expressed in this work are solely of the author
and do not necessarily reflect the views of the publisher,
who hereby disclaims any responsibility for them.

Copyright © 2024 Dr. Rebekah McCloud. All rights reserved.

No part of this book may be used or reproduced by any means,
graphic, electronic, or mechanical, including photocopying, recording,
taping, or by any information storage retrieval system without the
written permission of the publisher except in the case of brief
quotations embodied in critical articles and reviews.

Nuggets of Encouragement

Living Each Day with Grace & Love

Dr. Rebekah McCloud

Dedication

This book is dedicated to my parents, Rev. Arcollo McCloud, Sr., and Mrs. Ilean McCloud, who read and studied the Bible daily. They provided me with a firm Christian foundation and a strong work ethic. I still hold to these today. They anchored me and defined who I am and to whom I belong.

Acknowledgments

Thank you to Missionary Alice Jackson Gordon for serving as my proofreader. My dear sister in Christ, I appreciate your encouragement, eagle eyes, friendship, and time.

Thank you to Minister Charles Barfield, Esq. for the opportunity to start writing these nuggets. I appreciate your confidence in me and your constant encouragement.

Thank you to Pastor Tedd Washington (posthumously); he saw this book before I did. I appreciate his nudges and prayers.

Thank you to my family, friends, and the Grace for Living Ministries family. I appreciate your kind words, well wishes, prayers, and encouragement.

May God continue to bless all of you.

Note from the Author

The themes of this journal are love and grace. Throughout the Bible, we learn of God's love for us (John 3:16), his directions for us to love one another (John 13:34), and practical examples of love (1 Corinthians 13: 4-7). Simply put, God is love (1 John 4:8). His love surrounds us (Psalm 33:22), it surpasses knowledge (Ephesians 3:19), and it is everlasting (Jeremiah 31:3). Additionally, throughout the Bible we learn about God's grace. We know that grace is an unmerited gift God gives to us. Scriptures describe how he extends it to us (Ephesians 2: 4-5), the power of his grace (Titus 3: 4-7), and that it is freely given (Ephesians 1:6). In Him, we have our being (Acts 17:28) and receive grace upon grace (John 1:16).

This journal allows readers to consider their everyday lives from a fresh perspective. The real-life stories are anchored with scriptures to illustrate a point and for further studies. Each entry poses four questions for consideration. What are my key takeaways from this teaching is the first question. It allows readers to enumerate points that piqued their interest, resonated with them, or led them to study. The takeaways are different for each reader. Questions two and three are specific to each entry. There are no right or wrong answers. The questions provide readers with a vehicle by which they will give honest reflections. These questions are not a diagnostic or counseling tool. Accept them as food for thought. Question number four asks what are my next steps. It allows the reader to seek insight and God's direction in moving forward. The journal also includes opportunities for readers to recap and apply their learning.

God's love and grace are ever-present. They are two of the foundations upon which to build a victorious life. As you move through this journal, reflect on God's love, grace, and the practical application of both to your life. May this journal be a tool that enhances and strengthens your walk with God.

—Dr. Rebekah

Table of Contents

Aw, Snap	13
God's Promises	19
Let it Go	23
Stop, Drop, and Roll	27
Beware, the Thief	33
Unfailing Love	39
Grace Be unto You	45
Recap & Apply	49
Why Thank God?	51
A Seat at the Table	57
God Winks	61
Unapologetic Joy	65
Trust God	69
I Wish I Had Somebody	73
God's AI	79
Everybody Clean Up	83
Recap & Apply	89
Mission Possible	91
Things Old & New	95
Shout to the Lord	101

A Sweet Aroma: The Nose Knows 107
What's Love Got to Do with it?..111
Addition or Submission 115
What do I do with the Crumbs?..119
M.O.N.E.Y. 123
Recap & Apply..129

Aw, Snap

Recently I had some problems with my computer. It went on a blitz and alternated between blinking and being unresponsive. Suddenly an image appeared on the screen with a message beneath it that said, "Aw, snap. Something went wrong." Imagine that.

I asked several others if they had ever received this error message. Many said yes, so I searched the Internet to find out what to do when one gets this message. I scanned a dozen or so of the entries. Most of them had similar instructions. The three most common were to refresh the page, check the Internet connection, and reboot the system. Aw, snap! Like the computer, sometimes things go wrong in our lives. These solutions may work.

First, refresh. The word refresh means to give new strength or energy, rejuvenate, renew, reinvigorate, renovate, or restore. When something goes wrong in our lives—and believe me, even Christians have times of challenge—it is always best to stop and refresh. We are perfectly imperfect beings and are always in need of God's restoration. Acts 3:19 says, "Turn to God, so that your sins may be wiped out, that times of refreshing may come from the Lord." Psalm 19:7 reminds us, "The Law of the Lord is perfect, restoring the soul."

Refreshing may not always be spiritual; refreshing may come from fellowship such as that shared by the disciples and others (Philemon 1:7, 2 Corinthians 7:13, Isaiah 28:12, Romans 15:32). It may also be physical, sitting, enjoying a cup of coffee, meditating, reading your Bible, praying, etc. Refreshing provides us with the opportunity to focus and reflect.

Second, check your connection. The word connection means having a relationship with a person, place, or thing. Connecting with God is not just a Sunday event. It requires us to have continuing communications with him and that we prioritize our relationship with him. Put God first. Colossians 1:17 says, "He is before all things, and in Him all things hold together." He is the "Alpha and Omega, the First and the Last, the Beginning and the End," (Revelations 22:13).

Building and keeping that connection with God requires that we recognize that he is the vine and we are the branches (John 15:5). He gave us the right to become children of God (John 1:12). He loves us and is rich in mercy (Ephesians 2: 4-5). Let us plug into the source and have a solid, firm, concrete, rock-hard, unyielding connection with the father. "Seek the Lord and his strength, seek his face continually," (1 Chronicles 16:11).

Third, reboot. It means to shut down, clean up, and start something anew. When we give our lives to Christ or recommit our lives to Christ, we become new. 2 Corinthians 5:17 says in part, "Old things are passed away; behold, all things become new."

Isaiah 43:18-19 reminds us to, "Forget the former things; do not dwell on the past. See, I am doing a new thing! Now it springs up;

do you not perceive it? I am making a way in the wilderness and streams in the wasteland."

A reboot requires us to seek God's forgiveness, to seek his grace, to seek his restoration. He is eager for our return. As he did with the Israelites, he smooths out the roads, pulls out the boulders, raises a flag, and prepares the highway for our return (Isaiah 62:10). Our job then is to draw near to him; he will draw near to us (James 4:8).

Aw snap, we do not need an Internet search to find a solution to our problems. We can use something better; the Bible. The word of God has a solution to every problem known to man, from the beginning to the end. A friend sent me this quote of encouragement. "Look back and thank God. Look forward and trust God. He closes doors no man can open and he opens doors no man can close." Aw, snap! Something might have gone wrong, but the potter turns things around (Isaiah 29:16). We are all the work of his hand (Isaiah 64:8). Go to him to refresh, connect, and reboot.

Prayer

Lord, I need you. You are the potter; I am the clay. Guide me as I refresh, connect, and reboot to deepen my relationship with you. I will answer your knock at my door and stretch my hand to you. Amen.

Reflection

What are my key takeaways from this teaching?

In what ways do I need to refresh my connection with God?

When I go to God for a reboot, what should be my number one area of focus?

What are my next steps?

God's Promises

According to the Merriam-Webster Dictionary, promise is a declaration that one will do or refrain from doing something specified. It is also a legally binding declaration that gives the person to whom it is made a right to expect or to claim the performance or forbearance of a specified act. The word promise is found in the Bible 77 times. It is in the Old Testament and the New Testament. Wow! Something mentioned 77 times means it is important.

- God promised to bless Abraham (Genesis 12: 2-3)
- God promised Israel to be their God (Leviticus 26: 12-13)
- God promised we would find him if we searched for him (Deuteronomy 4:29)
- God promised to be with Joshua wherever he went (Joshua 1:9)
- God promised if we delighted in his word, he would bless us (Psalm 1: 1-3)
- God promised to protect his children (Psalm 121)

- God promised his love would never fail (1 Chronicles 16:34)
- God promised salvation to all who believed in him (Romans 1: 16-17)
- God promised that all things work together for our good (Romans 8:28)
- God promised peace when we pray (Philippians 4: 6-7)
- God promised to supply our needs (Matthew 6:33)
- Jesus promised to give us rest (Matthes 11:28)
- Jesus promised that he would return (John 14: 2-3)
- Jesus promised eternal life (John 4:14, John 10:28)
- Jesus promised believers that their names would not be blotted out of the Book of Life (Revelations 3:5)

As Christians, we have the right to the promises of God. "If you belong to Christ, then you are Abraham's seed, and heirs according to the promise," (Galatians 3:29). God did not have to promise us anything, nothing, nay thing, nada, not a drop; but he did. It is our job to hold fast to his unchanging hand. Romans 8:38-39 says, "For I am convinced that neither death, nor life, nor angels, nor principalities, nor things present, nor things to come, nor powers, nor height, nor depth, nor any other created thing, will be able to separate us from the love of God, which is in Christ Jesus our Lord." Amen, what a reminder of our connection with God and our ability to stand on the promises. "For I know the plans I have for you, declares the Lord, plans for welfare and not for evil, to give you a future and a hope," (Jeremiah 29:11).

2 Corinthians 1:20 says, "For no matter how many promises God has made, they are "Yes" in Christ. And so through him, the "Amen" is spoken by us to the glory of God." Hebrews 10:23 says, "Hold unswervingly to the hope we profess, for he who promised is

faithful." When I think about God's awesomeness and the promises he has made, I think about the many dreams I have, you have, and we have. If we know he will keep every promise and give us the desires of our hearts, it is our job to get busy praying and thanking God for his provision.

As you read your Bible, consider noting the promises of God. If we stand on the promises of God, we will run and not be weary, and according to 1 Peter 1: 4 we have, "an inheritance that can never perish, spoil or fade." God keeps every promise; let us claim one every day!

Prayer

Father, promise keeper, light in the darkness, thank you. You love me so much I can claim your promises. Like you did for Abraham and those before me, be with me. Keep my feet straight on the path and keep my mind on you. I am grateful for all you do. Amen.

Reflection

What are my key takeaways from this teaching?

Nuggets of Encouragement: Living Each Day with Grace & Love

What promise am I waiting for God to fulfill?

What promise do I need to make to God?

What are my next steps?

Let it Go

When I was a kid, each summer my family went on a fishing trip to the Saint Lawrence Seaway. My dad was a fisherman and one of his life's goals was to teach us to fish and to love it as much as he did. Afraid of the fish and the bait, Momma did not like to fish. But she was a good sport and she always tried.

One summer, while fishing, Momma caught an eel. When she pulled the eel out of the water, she thought it was a snake. She screamed, jumped up from her chair and started to run, fast! Unfortunately, she had a death grip on her pole. So, as she ran, the dangling eel would swing into her field of vision. Each time she saw the eel, she would scream again.

My dad, in fast pursuit, yelled, "Let it go. Let it go." Soon several other men joined the chase; they too yelled, "Let it go. Let it go." Eventually, Momma tired and stopped running. Dad caught up to her and wrestled the pole from her grip. That was the end of the fishing trip that summer.

How often are we like Momma? How often do we run fast tightly holding on to something we should have let go of some time ago? There are many things in our lives, in our hearts, on our minds, on our paths, and in our way, that keep us from being the good and faithful servants we are called to be. Most of the time we walk in the flesh, by sight and not by faith. When we walk by sight our vision is limited. When we think we have purchased on this slippery slope called life, we fall back into a hole and find that the thing we thought we had discarded is still tightly held in our grip.

To get out of the hole and run the race, there are a couple of things we need to do. First, release our grip and let it go. Hebrews 12:1 reminds us to, "Strip off every weight that slows us down, especially the sin that so easily trips us up. And let us run with endurance the race God has set before us." The second thing we need to do is to release our grip and let it go. Proverbs 4:25-26 says, "Look straight ahead and fix your eyes on what lies before you. Mark out a straight path for your feet; stay on the safe path." The third thing we need to do is to release our grip and let it go. 1 Corinthians 1:24 poses a question and gives a command. It says, "Don't you realize that in a race everyone runs, but only one person gets the prize? So run to win!"

We are all in a race and all have an "it." Sometimes it keeps us from having the very thing we desire. In 2 Kings (5: 1-15), Naaman, a mighty warrior and army commander had an "it." His "it" was pride. It almost kept him from being healed of leprosy. When he released his grip and let it go, he followed Elisha's instructions. He went down to the Jordan River, dipped himself seven times, and was healed. He released his grip and let it go. Amen.

We are all in a race and have an "it." To be victorious, we must trust God because he alone can keep us from falling. Psalm 46:10

says, "Be still, and know that I am God!" Isaiah 40:31 says, "But those who trust the Lord will find new strength. They will soar high on wings like eagles. They will run and not grow weary. They will walk and not faint."

We are all in a race and have an "it." Closed hands can do nothing nor can they receive anything. We must release our grip and let it go. Victory can be ours.

Prayer

Lord, help me to release my grip and let it go. Your word says, "Everything works together for the good of those who love God and are called according to his purpose." I am ready to run the race and trust you to lead me to victory. Amen.

Reflection

What are my key takeaways from this teaching?

What is my it?

What do I need to release from my grip?

What are my next steps?

Stop, Drop, and Roll

About half a century ago, I was a safety instructor (water safety, first aid, CPR, and fire safety). In the fire safety classes, we taught folk if they caught fire and wanted to extinguish it, they should stop, drop, and roll. Consider this thought, if you are committed to your walk with the Lord, you are on fire. Jerimiah 20:9, says the "fire [is] shut up in my bones." If you want to keep the Godly fire going, I encourage you to stop, drop, and roll.

First, stop negative talk, especially negative self-talk. Proverbs 18:21 says, "Death and life are in the power of the tongue, and they who indulge in it shall eat the fruit of it [for death or life]." We have heard this scripture many times, yet, as soon as we get a bad report from the doctor, we lose our jobs, our kids start acting up, or whatever, we start talking like Popeye's girlfriend, Olive Oyl, "Oh, woe is me!"

Let somebody cut us off in traffic or give us the stank eye; some of us will start the negative talk. Ephesians 4:29 tells us, "Let no foul *or* polluting language, *nor* evil word *nor* unwholesome *or* worthless talk [ever] come out of your mouth, but only such [speech] as is good *and* beneficial to the spiritual progress of others, as is fitting to the need *and* the occasion, that it may be a blessing *and* give grace (God's favor) to those who hear it." Let us remember what Matthew 12:36-37 says, "But I tell you, on the day of judgment men will have to give account for every idle (inoperative, nonworking) word they speak. For by your words, you will be justified *and* acquitted, and by your words, you will be condemned *and* sentenced." Amen. Let us learn to stop.

Second, in times of need, in times of doubt, in times of praise, and in times of thanksgiving, we should always drop to our knees and pray. Now that sounds simple, I know. But if I am honest, it is not always simple, at least not for me. Sometimes I start praying and my mind wanders off. I start thinking about everything but my prayer. Do you? 2 Corinthians 10:5 tells us to, "take captive every thought to make it obedient to Christ." Colossians 3:2 says, "Set your minds on things above, not earthly things." Philippians 4:8 says, "Finally, brothers and sisters, whatever is true, whatever is noble, whatever is right, whatever is pure, whatever is lovely, whatever is admirable— if anything is excellent or praiseworthy—think about such things. Amen. Let us learn to drop.

Third, no matter what, we need to roll. You have heard people say "Let's roll" and "roll with it." They use the word roll as an active action. In the Amplified, Proverbs 16:3 says, "Roll your works upon the Lord [commit and trust them wholly to Him; He will cause your thoughts to become agreeable to His will, and] so shall your plans be established *and* succeed. In the NIV, it says, "Commit to the Lord whatever you do, and he will establish your plans." Psalm 37:5 says, "Commit your way to the Lord; trust in him and he will do this." There is one last thing we need to do to roll with the Lord.

Romans 12:1 says "to offer [our] bodies as a living sacrifice, holy and pleasing to God." Amen. Let us learn to roll.

My nephew, Shawn, posted a very touching thought, a personal testimony on his Facebook page. I want to share it with you. He wrote:

"My faith will not be dictated nor defined by my struggles. Notwithstanding, my perceived failures or triumphs, I shall remain at peace, with self-control and balanced emotional discipline. I praise God for I am patiently humbled by absolute trust in Him and the process of His plan. My faith has been planted into an indestructible foundation of love for God. I may be shaken, but I will not break. I may be down, but I am not out. With God, I am rising and will stand a better man than when I fell. These are not simply sweet ideas; this is not just a ploy. God has moved me into action, springing me toward Him with a throttling sprint! Gitty, elated to chase him, trusting Him."

Amen, what a testimony to the wonder-working power of the Lord. And what an example of how we can stop, drop, and roll.

Prayer

Father, the song says great are you Lord, greatly to be praised. Lord, touch our minds our bodies, and our spirits. Guide us, show us when to stop, drop, and roll. Renew us and allow us to be the good and faithful servants you require of us. Father, you reign! Amen.

Reflection

What are my key takeaways from this teaching?

What things do I need to stop or drop?

Am I ready to roll with God?

What are my next steps?

Beware, the Thief

I recently read an article that talked about social media and social comparison. Researchers are finding that it can lead to depression, anxiety, poor self-esteem, poor body image, envy, and other things. The number of followers and likes people have on their social media platforms is often used as a measuring stick to define their self-worth. Even Christians are falling into this comparison trap.

Theodore Roosevelt once said, "Comparison is the thief of joy." Comparing ourselves to others puts us in a negative frame of mind. It can bring on feelings of lowliness, inferiority, subservience, and inadequacy. It can also stir greed, bitterness, resentment, envy, and jealousy within us. Our human nature has us look across the fence to see what we perceive as greener grass, but it is just green.

Although we compare, we should not. We are distinct individuals, each created by God in His image. God was intentional when he created each of us. He gave each of us a unique gift. Romans 12: 6-8 says, "We have different gifts, according to the grace given to each of us. If your gift is prophesying, then prophesy in accordance with your faith; if it is serving, then serve; if it is teaching, then teach; if it is to encourage, then give encouragement; if it is giving, then give generously; if it is to lead, do it diligently; if it is to show mercy, do it cheerfully." 1 Peter 4:10 tells us, "as each has received a gift, use it to serve one another, as good stewards of God's varied grace."

So, let us be clear. We are distinct individuals made in God's image with a unique gift. Right? So why all the fuss about comparison; is it much ado about nothing? Comparison has been around for a long time. If we go to the first book of the Bible, Genesis, we will find Cain & Able (Genesis 4:2-16). This is one of the first stories about comparison. Both brothers gave an offering to the Lord. The Lord found favor in Abel's offering but did not find favor in Cain's. Cain grew angry, lured his brother out to the field, and killed him. There are other stories: Leah and Rachel (Genesis 29:15-35, 30:1-24), The Prodigal Son (Luke 15:11-32), and Joseph and his brothers (Genesis 37:3-4, 18-25), for instance. In each story, envy reared its ugly head. Proverbs 14:30 says, "A tranquil heart gives life to the flesh, but envy makes the bones rot."

The Bible is very clear about comparison. Consider these verses.

- Galatians 6:4 says, "Pay careful attention to your own work, for then you will get the satisfaction of a job well done, and you won't need to compare yourself to anyone else."
- 2 Corinthians 10:12 cautions, "Not that we dare to classify or compare ourselves with some of those who are commending themselves. But when they measure themselves by one another and compare themselves with one another, they are without understanding."
- James 3:16 says "For wherever there is jealousy and selfish ambition, there you will find disorder and evil of every kind."

- Colossians 3:23 reminds us, "Whatever you do, work heartily, as for the Lord and not for men."
- Isaiah 2:22 warns, "Stop regarding man in whose nostrils is breath, for of what account is he?"
- 1 Corinthians 11:1 says, "Be imitators of me, as I am of Christ."

Genesis 1:16 points out the matchlessness of God's creations. It says, "God made the two great lights, the greater light to govern the day, and the lesser light to govern the night; He made the stars also." Each was unique and had its job. In the six days of his labor, God was intentional, purposeful, and decisive in his design. He made no mistakes.

We are just what God planned; for whom and through whom everything was made. We are good enough, more than enough. Let us guard our minds and our hearts against comparison. Let us pray for those over whom comparison has a stronghold. Let us mark our doorposts with the blood of Jesus so that comparison does not creep in like a thief in the night and devour us. Remember, to Him who is able, all things are possible.

Prayer

Lord, I am so glad that I was intentionally and deliberately made. I am a unique individual with a unique purpose and a unique fingerprint. Thank you for leading me in the plans and purposes you designed uniquely for me. Amen.

Reflection

What are my key takeaways from this teaching?

Am I allowing comparisons to creep into areas of my life?

What are some ways I can use my God-given uniqueness?

What are my next steps?

Unfailing Love

Recently, I took a tumble and had to elevate my leg and place an ice pack on it several times daily. To entertain myself during these periods, I decided to watch TV. I am not much of a TV watcher so I was a little surprised at the number of shows centered around the same topic—love. It seems like many people are looking for love. To love and to be loved is human nature. Remember, God thought Adam should not be alone so God created Eve and gave her to Adam (Genesis 1: 18-24). Since that time, humans have been seeking to find the one that was made just for them. So many have worked for their Rachel (Genesis 29) or waited for their Boaz (Ruth 2 -4).

Just what is this thing called love? According to Bible Gateway, the word love appears 686 times in the New International Version (NIV) of the Bible. It appears 425 times in the Old Testament and 261 times in the New Testament. There are four types of love in the Bible. There is Eros (romantic love), Storge (family love), Philia (brotherly love), and Agape (God's divine love). At some point, most people experience all four types of love. First, we should seek the Agape kind of love; put God first. The steadfast love of the Lord never ceases (Lamentations 3:22).

Love is a word that when spoken, almost everybody can think of one person or thing that they love. We love our spouses, children, and families; our jobs, homes, and cars; our lifestyles, our food, our clothes; our pastors, and our churches. We are a nation of "lovers." Or are we? When you love God with all your heart, your strength, your soul, and your being, you cannot help but pass the joy onto others.

The book of Psalms contains many verses that remind us of God's unfailing love. Here are a few to consider:

- Psalm 13:5—But I trust in your unfailing love; my heart rejoices in your salvation.
- Psalm 31:16—Let your face shine on your servant; save me in your unfailing love.
- Psalm 33: 5—The LORD loves righteousness and justice; the earth is full of His unfailing love.
- Psalm 33:22—May your unfailing love be with us, LORD, even as we put our hope in you.
- Psalm 36: 7—How priceless is your unfailing love, O God! People take refuge in the shadow of your wings.
- Psalm 40:11—LORD, do not hold back your tender mercies from me. Let your unfailing love and faithfulness always protect me.
- Psalm 48:9—O God, we meditate on your unfailing love as we worship in your Temple.
- Psalm 90: 14—Satisfy us in the morning with your unfailing love, that we may rejoice and be glad all our days
- Psalm 94:18—When I said, "My foot is slipping," your unfailing love, LORD, supported me.

- Psalm 143:8—Let the morning bring me word of your unfailing love, for I have put my trust in you. Show me the way I should go, for to you I entrust my life.

God's love is unfailing. Remember, God loves us so much that if we delight ourselves in the Lord, God will give us the desires of our hearts. We must stop looking for love in all the wrong places and look up! God is faithful. God knows the plans he has for us and God wants to give us good and perfect gifts.

Our job is simple. First, we must stop being afraid. There is no fear in love (I John 4:18). Second, we must allow God to prepare us for what God has prepared for us. If a husband or a wife, a King or a Queen, an Eve or a Rachel, or a Boaz or a Joseph is one of the desires of your heart, do not fret, count it done. God's promises are true and God's unfailing love for us endures forever.

Prayer

God, thank you for your unfailing love. You love us so much that you gave your son Jesus in remission of our sins. For this gift, I am eternally grateful. May I be found worthy of your sacrifice and your love. Amen

Reflection

What are my key takeaways from this teaching?

What challenges do I have in finding love?

How do I show love in a Godly way?

What are my next steps?

Grace Be unto You

Lately, the word grace has been ruminating in my spirit. The dictionary says that grace is undeserved favor. Grace is a powerful thing that we all need. I need it every day. There is so much that distracts us, that demands our attention, and that causes us to shake our heads. At times, these might cause us to act out of character or even cause us to question our faith. At any of these times, we must remember that God's grace is sufficient to take us through and to keep us. 2 Timothy 1:9 tells us that, "He [God] has saved us and called us to a holy life—not because of anything we have done but because of his purpose and grace. This grace was given us in Christ Jesus before the beginning of time." John 1:17 reminds us of the origin of grace. It reads, "The law was given through Moses; grace and truth came through Jesus Christ."

The Bible is filled with people who benefitted from God's grace. There are too many to mention, but here is a partial list: Noah, Abraham, Daniel, Rahab, Moses, the Israelites, Joseph, Ruth, Esther, and Job. Additionally, this thing called grace may be found in all 66 books of the Bible. Each passage provides us with a glimpse of God's goodness and grace. Here are a few examples to get you started.

- Numbers— God shows his grace by sustaining a grumbling people.
- Joshua— God shows his grace by giving Israel victory in its conquests.
- Nehemiah—God shows grace in rebuilding the walls of the city.
- Amos—God shows grace in promising restoration.
- Obadiah—God's grace is shown by delivering judgment on Edom.
- Habakkuk— God shows his grace by giving it freely; it costs nothing.
- Luke—God's grace is extended to all regardless of their station.
- Romans—God gives grace to the ungodly.
- 2 Corinthians—God's grace is manifested through weakness rather than strength.
- Colossians—God's grace is shown by nailing our sins to the cross.
- Titus—God shows his grace by saving us by his cleansing mercy.
- 1 Peter —God shows his grace by securing an inheritance for us.
- 1 John —God shows his grace by adopting us as his children.
- Revelations—God shows his grace by preserving us through tribulation.

From Genesis to Revelations, grace may be found. Romans 3:23-24 is a clarion call. It says, "For all have sinned and fall short of the glory of God, and all are justified freely by his grace through the redemption that came by Christ Jesus." Grace be unto you.

Prayer

Lord, may I be found worthy of a measure of your grace. Thank you for working with me, talking with me, and preparing me for your service. Amen.

Reflection

What are my key takeaways from this teaching?

How have I benefitted from God's grace?

To whom or in what situation do I need to extend grace?

What are my next steps?

Recap & Apply

What have I learned about God's love?

How will I apply this learning to my life?

What have I learned about God's grace?

How will I apply this learning to my life?

Why Thank God?

We all have challenges in our lives. Sometimes there is sunshine and sometimes there is rain. My Dad used to say, "Every day cannot be Sunday." You might ask, why would a loving God allow suffering in our lives? I ask, why not? When we became Christian followers of Christ, our walk did not come with an invisible force field. Instead, it came with the Word and love of God.

The way we handle the challenges of our lives depends solely on how we handle our lives in times when we are not in crisis. Our lives should be full of thanksgiving. Hannah had it right; 1 Samuel 2:1-2 was her song of thankfulness to God. She did not ask God for anything, she thanked him.

So, you might ask, why thank God? God is a loving father who cares so much for us that he provides for our every need. He knows the number of hairs on our heads. He knows our concerns, hopes, dreams, and desires. He knows our weaknesses and our strengths. He is the reason that we exist.

He hears our cries. He gives us joy. He endures our pain. He gives us strength. He hears our prayers. He will never leave us. He is our comforter, our rock, our shield. He is the mighty physician, our constant companion, our savior, and our friend.

So, you might ask, why thank God? I ask, why not? Thank him day in and day out. He is worthy of our thanks. The Bible is filled with many reasons why we should thank God. Use it as your guide. Here are a few scriptures to get you started.

- Give thanks in all circumstances; for this is the will of God in Christ Jesus for you. --1 Thessalonians 5:18
- Continue steadfastly in prayer, being watchful in it with thanksgiving. --Colossians 4:2
- Give thanks to the LORD of hosts, for the LORD is good, for his steadfast love endures forever!'--Jeremiah 33:11
- I will give thanks to the LORD with my whole heart; I will recount all your wonderful deeds. --Psalm 9:1
- Oh, give thanks to the LORD, for he is good; for his steadfast love endures forever! --1 Chronicles 16:34
- Be careful for nothing; but in everything by prayer and supplication with thanksgiving let your requests be made known unto God. --Philippians 4:6
- Through Him, let us continually offer a sacrifice of praise to God, that is, the fruit of lips that give thanks to His name. --Hebrew 13:15
- Oh, give thanks to the LORD, for He is good, For His lovingkindness is everlasting. --Psalm 107:1
- "We give You thanks, O Lord God, the Almighty, who are and who were because You have taken Your great power and have begun to reign. --Revelations 11:17

The next time you have challenges, know that God has already equipped you with all you need. Romans 5:3 reminds us, "We can rejoice, too, when we run into problems and trials, for we know that they help us develop endurance." James 1:12 tells us to "Consider it pure joy, my brothers and sisters, whenever you face trials of many kinds." Verse 12 concludes, "Blessed is the one who perseveres under trial because, having stood the test, that person will receive the crown of life that the Lord has promised to those who love him." Thank God for the trials, and even more, for endurance. Like Hannah, thank Him.

Prayer

Lord, Jesus, thank you for the way that you love us. Thank you for the trials and tribulations you bring into our lives. Each of these provides us a testimony and an opportunity to say thanks. We bless you and we honor you. Amen

Reflection

What are my key takeaways from this teaching?

What is something for which I need to thank God?

How can I thank God even in a time of challenge?

What are my next steps?

A Seat at the Table

My dad used to say that to get a seat at the table, you must be in the room. So many folks miss their opportunity because they are outside peeping in the window. That makes me think about our Christian walk. Are we missing out on God's promises? Are we forfeiting our seat at God's table? Are we peeping in or out of the window, standing in the room, or sitting at the table?

Most of us have had trials and tribulations in our lives. We have had health issues, setbacks, losses, heartbreaks, disappointments, and so on. Some of us have overcome; others are still battling. God never promised us a life free from struggle. He promised He would leave His peace with us (John 14:27). He promised He would give us perfect peace (Isaiah 26:3), He would give us rest (Matthew 11:28), and that His grace would be sufficient for us (2 Corinthians 12:9). He promised to be our refuge and our shield (1 Corinthians 10:13). He promised to guard us from the evil one (2 Thessalonians 3:3).

Be assured that God will not to be slow about His promises (2 Peter 3:9). If we endure, guaranteed, we will receive what was promised (Hebrew 10:36). Psalm 77:8 asks, "Has His lovingkindness ceased forever? Has His promise come to an end forever?" I say a resounding no! Just as it was for Israel (Old Testament), it can be for us. Joshua 21:45 reports that "not one of the good promises which the Lord had made to the house of Israel failed; all came to pass." Romans 4:21 tells us to be, "fully convinced that God was able to do what He had promised." His promises are yes and Amen (2 Corinthians 1:20).

I hear the skeptics. Yeah, but. So what? Now what? Peace, be still. Several ministers have talked about people having a bad case of the "Can't Help It." Here is my take on it. Some of us cannot help doubting. Some cannot help worrying. Some cannot help fearing, and some cannot help their unbelief. We just cannot help it.

Consider this for a moment, is there anything too hard for God? Indeed, He will finish what He started. If He can do a new thing for Moses, He can do it for us. Revelations 21:5 says, "Behold, I am making all things new." Sometimes, we must get out of our way and stop peeping in the window so we cannot help but trust. We cannot help but believe, we cannot help but know, and we cannot help but rejoice. Hallelujah!

There is room at God's table for all of us. His grace is more than sufficient. He stands at the door and knocks. It is time to stop peeping out the window and let Him in.

Prayer

Lord, help us to remember that there is always room for us at your table. Your favor, your grace, and your love for us are more than enough. Your death on the cross reminds us of your unfailing love for us. Amen

Reflection

What are my key takeaways from this teaching?

What opportunity am I missing? Have I claimed my seat at God's table?

What can't I help? What assistance do I need?

What are my next steps?

God Winks

Recently, I had a challenging day. Some things I had planned fell apart. As I sat with myself, my dad came to mind. He was a Baptist preacher and a pastor who passed away in 1979. Yet, I can still hear his voice. When my siblings and I had a bad day, my father would listen intently, console us, and then place one of his big hands on our heads and pray for us. After that, he would give us the "God Winks" talk.

He would tell us to "talk to God about the situation. God knows all about it. He knew you before your momma did. Now when you are talking to God, you must listen more than you talk. To listen, you must hush, shut up, and be quiet. God sometimes whispers. Now, do not try to bargain with God or make any promises. Listen, be obedient, and watch God work. Man plans and God winks." Wise words.

God knows us. He knows us better than anyone, including ourselves. In Jeremiah 1:5, God says, "Before I formed you in the womb, I knew you." Psalm 139:13 says, "You made all the delicate, inner parts of my body and knit me together in my mother's womb." He knows all about us.

God speaks, we need to listen. Sometimes the busyness and the noisiness of our lives make it hard to hear. Psalm 46:10 says, "Be still and know that I am God." 1 King 19:12, says God spoke in a "still, small voice." Often, God speaks in silence. We must learn to listen.

God does not bargain. Matthew 7:7 (MSG) says, "Do not bargain with God. Be direct. Ask for what you need." Proverbs 20:25 says, "It is a trap to dedicate something rashly and only later to consider one's vows." Remember Jephthah's bargain with God (Judges 11: 29-40)? God does not need our bargains. God wants our obedience. In John 14:15, Jesus says, "If you love me, you will obey what I command." 1 Samuel 15:22 says, "To obey is better than sacrifice." God rewards those who obey. In the Old Testament, the Israelites are a good example of those who were rewarded. Their hard-headedness caused some delay, but in the end, He was faithful.

God winks. Our humanness sometimes leads us to believe we have everything under control; we have got this! Truth be known, our plans are moot to God. Proverbs 19:21 says, "Many plans are in man's heart, but the counsel of the Lord will stand." Proverbs 16:19 says, "The mind of man plans his way, But the Lord directs his steps." Acts 17:30, in part, tells us, "And the times of this ignorance, God winked." Finally, Psalm 94:11 says, "The Lord knows the thoughts of man, that they are a mere breath."

If we consult God, listen to Him, and obey Him, we can see God's work. Jeremiah 29:11 tells us, "For I know the plans I have for you," declares the Lord, "plans to prosper you and not to harm you, plans to give you hope and a future." Good days, bad days, plans or not, we are in good hands. God has got this! Be still and know He is God.

Prayer

Lord, thank you for the opportunity to know you. Continue to speak into my life and wink when necessary. Amen

Reflection

What are my key takeaways from this teaching?

What situation do I need to talk about with God?

In what ways have I been trying to bargain with God?

What are my next steps?

Unapologetic Joy

Last December, in recognition of the Christmas season, I bought two white, wooden cutouts with the word joy written on them. I placed them outside my house on either side of my front porch door. When the holiday was over, I decided to leave them there. I had a challenging year and by the grace of God, I made it through, triumphantly. As a result, I resolved to choose joy, embrace joy, live with joy, and be unapologetically joyful. Joy is a choice.

The dictionary says joy is a feeling of great pleasure and happiness and a source or cause of delight. The Apostle Paul defines joy as one of the fruits of the spirit. Galatians 5:22-23 says, "But the fruit of the Spirit is love, joy, peace, patience, kindness, goodness, faithfulness, gentleness, self-control; against such things, there is no law."

Joy is a choice. It is plentiful, free, and ours to choose. Romans 15:13 says, "May the God of hope fill you with all joy and peace in believing, so that by the power of the Holy Spirit you may abound in hope." What a promise! God will fill us with joy and peace.

The word joy appears in the Old Testament 93 times. Here are a few of my favorites.
- Proverbs 17:22 "A joyful heart is good medicine."
- Psalm 16: 11 "You make known to me the path of life; in your presence there is fullness of joy."
- Proverbs 10:28 "The hope of the righteous brings joy."
- Psalm 97:11 "Light is sown for the righteous, and joy for the upright in heart."
- Psalm 51:12 "Restore to me the joy of your salvation, and uphold me with a willing spirit."
- Psalm 30: 5 "Weeping may tarry for the night, but joy comes with the morning."
- Psalm 126: 5 "Those who sow in tears shall reap with shouts of joy!"

We can find joy. Life is not always easy; there are challenges and victories, hills and valleys, deserts, and oases. Through it all, the Lord is with us. Every mountain top is within reach if we keep climbing. A river cuts through a rock not because of its power, but its persistence. Nehemiah 8:10 says, "The joy of the Lord is my strength." Be unapologetic. Choose joy!

Prayer

Lord, I am grateful that you are the center of my joy. Assist me to walk in your presence and your eternal joy. Amen.

Reflection

What are my key takeaways from this teaching?

Is my life filled with joy? Why/why not?

How can I share joy with others?

What are my next steps?

Trust God

When I was in high school, my English teacher told us there were four words we needed to eliminate from our vocabulary—so, many, little, and thing. She said they did not add anything to a conversation or a description. They are fluff and filler words. There are two words I believe should eliminated from Christian vocabulary—try and cannot. They are in opposition to what the Bible says we can and we will do in Christ Jesus. The dictionary says the word try means to make an attempt or effort to do something. It says the word cannot is to be unable to do otherwise. Try and cannot do sound like Christ-like actions. Do they?

The Bible is full of promises from God. My English teachers would not like this sentence, but there are so many little things the Bible says we will do, not try to do, but will do if we remember two words: Trust God. Are you having issues with haters? The Bible says we will be victorious; not try to or cannot be, but we will be victorious because he will make our enemies our footstool. Trust God. Do you have some areas in your life where the enemy might get a toehold? James 4:7 says, "Resist the devil, and he will flee from you." It did not say try to or cannot do; it says resist and he will flee. Trust God. Have negative thoughts or negative words filled your heart or clouded your vision? You can overcome them. Proverbs 18:21 says, "Death and life are in the power of the tongue and those who love it will eat its fruits." It did not say we should try or could not eat; it said we would eat. Trust God. Are you overwhelmed, weak, weary, or afraid? Do not be. You can find refuge; the Lord is with you. Isaiah 41:10 says, "Fear not, for I am your God; I will strengthen you, I will help you, I will uphold you with my righteous right hand." The scripture did not say I am going to try to nor did it say I cannot do. Three times it said God will do it. I will strengthen you; I will help you; I will uphold you. Trust God.

So, what does the Bible say about trusting God? Psalms says, "Commit your way to the Lord; trust in him, and he will act," (Psalm 37:5). "Those who know your name put their trust in you," (Psalm 9:10). "Some trust in chariots and some in horses, but we trust in the name of the Lord our God," (Psalm 20:7). "It is better to take refuge in the Lord than to trust in man," (Psalm 118:8). Finally, Proverbs 3:5-6 says, "Trust in the Lord with all your heart and lean not on your own understanding. In all your ways acknowledge him, and he will make straight your paths."

We do not have to try to do it, God will help us. He is our strong tower, our protection, and our strength. He that began a good work in us, will bring it to completion. Let us stop trying to and saying we cannot do a thing; do it. Remember the two words: Trust God.

Prayer

Father, the great I am, thank you. By your leadership, I can do more than I ever thought possible. You are the God of I can. Like Paul, I believe that I can do all things through Christ who strengthens me. Amen.

Reflection

What are my key takeaways from this teaching?

What am I struggling with that so far, I cannot do?

What will I trust God to enable me to do?

What are my next steps?

I Wish I Had Somebody

My father, the Rev. Dr., was a Baptist minister, pastor, and denominational leader. I loved to hear him preach. He had a deep voice like James Earl Jones and was a natural-born storyteller. He could take one scripture and turn it into a 45-minute sermon. I loved him dearly. As a young girl, I would sneak into his room and watch him prepare his sermons. He would usually have four or five translations of the Bible, Strong's Concordance, and a couple of notebooks strewn about. He would write and erase and talk and pace and pray. On Sunday, he would deliver his sermon in a call-and-response fashion. He would say, "I wish I had somebody."

I used to wonder what he meant. As I got older, the meaning became clear. I wish I had somebody who understands the goodness of the Lord, the power of the Lord, the mercy, the grace, and the blessings of the Lord. I wish I had somebody who could testify with me and share their story of triumph.

God is Jehovah Rapha, the one who heals (Exodus 15:26). The Bible says God can provide four kinds of healing (physical, emotional, mental, and spiritual). At some point, many of us have needed some healing. The Song of Solomon 16:12 tells us that the word of God heals all things. Many scriptures attest to God's ability and desire to heal our physical bodies. Jeremiah 17:14 says, "Heal me, Lord, and I will be healed." Exodus 23:25 reminds us to worship the Lord and he will take away the sickness from among us. Jeremiah says, God will restore health (Jeremiah 30:17) and he will bring health and healing (Jeremiah 33:6). Finally, Psalms 41:3 tells us that, "The Lord sustains them on their sickbed and restores them from their bed of illness." God is also able to heal us emotionally. Psalm 34:18 says, "The Lord is close to the brokenhearted; he rescues those whose spirits are crushed." Psalm 147: 3 echoes that by saying, "He heals the brokenhearted and binds up their wounds." God has been my healer, Jehovah Rapha, many, many times. By His grace, I do not look like what I have been through. Amen! I wish I had somebody who could testify and share their story about God's healing power.

God is Jehovah Jireh, our provider. At some point, many of us have needed God's provision. The Bible tells us that God provided for the Israelites for the 40 years they wandered in the wilderness; they lacked for nothing (Deuteronomy 2:7). Psalm 147:8 says, God "covers the sky with clouds; he supplies the earth with rain and makes grass grow on the hills." Additionally, God feeds the birds of the air who do not reap or sow, are we not more valuable than them (Matthew 6:26)? God knows everything, not some of the things, but all that we need. If we trust him, he will meet all our needs (Philippians 4:19). We must be sure to do as Psalm 37:4 says and delight ourselves in the Lord and he will give us the desires of our hearts. "Eye has not seen, nor ear heard, nor have entered into the heart of man the things which God has prepared for those who love

Him," (1 Corinthians 2:9). God has been Jehovah Jireh and provided for me repeatedly. I wish I had somebody who could testify and share their story about God's provision.

God is Jehovah Shalom, our peace. In a world that is crowded with noise and distractions of all sorts, at some point, many of us have needed God's peace. Isaiah 26:3 tells us that God will keep us in perfect peace. Colossians 3:15 reminds us to let the peace of Christ rule in our hearts. We are told to cast all our cares on the Lord (1 Peter 5:7) and not to be anxious about anything (Philippians 4:6) for the God of peace will be with us (Romans 15:33). Peace is one of the fruits of the spirit discussed in Galatians 5:22. One of my favorite passages in the Bible concerning peace is in John 14:27. During a gathering with the disciples, Jesus reassured them by saying, "Peace I leave with you, my peace I give to you; not as the world gives do I give to you. Let not your heart be troubled, neither let it be afraid." What a wonderful promise. No matter what, the Lord's peace is always with us. God has been Jehovah Shalom, my peace, and calmed the waters for me when the seas were raging. I wish I had somebody who could testify and share their story about God's peace. Oh, I wish I had somebody!

Prayer

God, I am so thankful for your grace and mercy. To paraphrase an unknown author, "Be above us to bless us, below us to support us, before us to guide us, behind us to protect us, beside us to comfort us, and inside us to give us strength and joy." Amen.

Reflection

What are my key takeaways from this teaching?

What is an area of need that God can fill for me?

What is an area of healing (physical, emotional, mental, or spiritual) that God can provide for me?

What are my next steps?

God's AI

Artificial Intelligence (AI) has been around since 1956. In the last decade, it has advanced and become integrated into our daily technological functioning. I saw an advertisement the other day about AI. The caption said, "reinvent what's possible." Now that was one of those things that made me say hmmm. Isn't that an aspect of the power of God? In the Message Bible, Psalm 77:14 says, "You're the God who makes things happen; you showed everyone what you can do."

The Bible is full of examples of what God can do. God parted the Red Sea and let the Israelites cross on dry land to escape Pharaoh's Army (Exodus 14: 21-22). God provided the widow with a never-ending jar of flour and jug of oil (I Kings 17: 14-16). God allowed a donkey to speak to Balaam (Numbers 22:28-30). God gave extraordinary strength to Elijah to outrun Ahab's chariots (I Kings 18:46). God stopped the earth from spinning so the Israelites could defeat their enemies (Joshua 10:13). God placed Jesus in Mary's womb (Luke 1:27-35). Nothing is too hard for God. Did he not reinvent what is possible?

Then came Jesus. He did many things as well. John 21:25 says, "…If every one of them was written down, I suppose that even the whole world would not have room for the books that would be written." In addition to healing people and feeding the masses, Jesus turned water into wine (John 2: 1-11). Jesus cast out an unclean spirit (Mark 1: 23-28). Jesus opened blind eyes (Matthew 9: 27-31, John 9: 1-38, and Mark 8: 22-26). He raised people from the dead (John 11: 1-46, Luke 7: 11-18, and Matthew 9: 18-26). Did he not reinvent what is possible?

There is no reason to doubt that the father and the son can do what seems impossible. They can call those things that are not as if they were (Romans 4:17). Isaiah 60:22 tells us that when the time is right, the Lord will make things happen. We do not need to wonder what if. Jesus asks in Mark 9:23, "If? There are no ifs among believers. Anything can happen."

God is greater than artificial intelligence. He is great and greatly to be praised (Psalm 96:4). There is none like our God. He has done things that seemed like they were impossible in my life. He may have done so for you. God specializes in what seems to be impossible. Man cannot fathom His power. 1 Corinthians 2:9 says, "Eye has not seen, nor ear heard, nor have entered into the heart of man the things which God has prepared for those who love him." Ephesians 3:20 says God can do, "Exceedingly, abundantly, above all that we ask or think."

God has a plan and a purpose for our lives. This plan is crafted for each of us and is full of possibilities and God's AI (awesome impact). It is up to us to keep our eyes focused on the Master. Micah 6:8 tells us that God requires three things of us: to act justly, to love mercy, and to walk humbly. When we follow God's lead, all things are possible, even those that seem impossible. God's awesome impact (AI) will ripple through our lives like a pebble thrown into a pond. He is able! My God is awesome, awesome, awesome, awesome.

Prayer

God, you have made an awesome impact in my life. I am not what I used to be. I see your hand leading me, polishing me, and perfecting me day by day. Thank you. You are awesome! Amen.

Reflection

What are my key takeaways from this teaching?

How has God reinvented what is possible in my life?

Do I know the plan God has for my life?

What are my next steps?

Everybody Clean Up

Tucked between the pages of one of Momma's Bibles was a sheet from a 1982 publication. On it was a poem titled "Door of My Heart." The words of the anonymous author spoke to me 42 years later.

The first stanza of the poem reads as follows:

> *"God knocked at the door of my heart one day*
> *And I looked for a place to hide.*
> *My soul was cluttered and choked with debris*
> *And things were untidy inside."*

I do not know about you all, but I have some clutter. Sometimes it is overwhelming. I have too much stuff: my stuff and my family's stuff. I have been cleaning for several months; I still have stuff. Lately, this stuff has occupied a lot of time and takes me away from other things. If I am honest with myself, in many ways my behavior is like that of the rich man in Luke 12:16-21 who stores up things.

I have decided to heed the warning of Luke 12:15, "Watch out! Be on your guard against all kinds of greed; life does not consist in an abundance of possessions." I do not want God to knock and find my life filled with clutter and choked with debris.

When our kids were small and had stuff everywhere, to signal it was time to tidy up, I would sing, "Clean up, clean up, everybody everywhere; clean up clean up, everybody does your share!" Is it time for the clean-up song?

The poem's second stanza says:

> *"I needed some time to put matters right*
> *Surprised He would call on me.*
> *My soul needed cleaning from bottom to top*
> *There were things he should not see."*

Are there things in our lives God should not see? Being a Christian does not mean that we are perfect. None is but He. However, be reminded of 2 Timothy 2:15. It says, "Do your best to present yourself to God as one approved, a worker who does not need to be ashamed and who correctly handles the word of truth." Our Christian walk should be just that simple.

But we walk in the flesh, in the natural. And as humans, sometimes we allow the flesh to override the spirit. This is not a new thing. Just ask David. After he committed adultery with Bathsheba, he cried out to God for forgiveness. In Psalm 51:10 he said, "Create in me a pure heart, O God, and renew a steadfast spirit within me." There may come a time that because of our actions, we must ask God the same. Are there things in our lives God should not see? Is it time for the clean-up song?

The third stanza reads:

> *"There were tasks neglected, long overdue*
> *Cobwebs to be brushed from the wall,*
> *Rugs to be shaken and windows cleaned up.*
> *I had not expected this call."*

Are we ready for God's call? Are there things we have neglected to do? Have we been the kind of stewards God has called us to be? Have we been mindful of the Great Commission and the Ten Commandments? Have we made Jesus our choice? Whether the answers are yes or no, Matthew 24:44 reminds us, "So you also must be ready, because the Son of Man will come at an hour when you do not expect him." 1 Peter 3:15 in part says, "But in your hearts revere Christ as LORD. Always be prepared to answer everyone who asks you to give the reason for the hope that you have." And, Luke 12:35 tells us to "Be dressed, ready for service, and keep your lamps burning." Are we ready for God's call? Is it time for the clean-up song?

Finally, the fourth stanza says:

> *"I stood up with my hand on the latch of the door*
> *And gazed at the mess in the room.*
> *When I opened the door, my soul blushed to see*
> *God had left on my doorstep—a broom."*

If God left us a broom, what things would we sweep out of our lives? Gossiping, waste, lack, busyness, devices, or SIN: self-inflected nonsense…you name it. Whatever it is, let us sweep it out. We must be, got to be stewards that God can use. Joshua 3:5 tells us to "Consecrate yourselves, for tomorrow the LORD will do amazing things among you." 2 Timothy 2:21 says, "Those who cleanse themselves from the latter will be instruments for special purposes, made holy, useful to the Master and prepared to do any good work." Is it time for the clean-up song? God, please leave us a broom.

Prayer

Lord, thank you for the broom. Allow me to sweep out those things that are not of you. I trust you and know that you have plans for me. Make me ready to be used by you and to receive what you have for me. Amen.

Reflection

What are my key takeaways from this teaching?

Where do I have clutter that needs addressing?

Which stanza of the poem resonates with me? Why?

What are my next steps?

Recap & Apply

What have I learned about God's love?

How will I apply this learning to my life?

What have I learned about God's grace?

How will I apply this learning to my life?

Mission Possible

Back in the 1960s, there was a TV show called Mission Impossible. The opening included three famous sentences. Sentence one said: Your mission Jim, should you choose to accept it. Jim never said no, uh-uh, no way, not living, slow your roll, pump your breaks, or as one of my staff members says, "You must be crazy mommy." He never said no. He always accepted the mission. What I liked about the show was that Jim had a team. Each had a role to play and they had the tools they needed to be successful. Now equate this to our Christian walk. God gives us the mission, defines our roles, provides us with tools, and guarantees our success.

Our mission as Christians on God's team is to be a manager of those things God has put under our control: our time, our talent, and our resources. Our role on God's team is to act justly and to love mercy and to walk humbly with your God, (Micah 6:8). Simple? Perhaps. Some of us struggle with these actions: to act justly, to love mercy, and to walk humbly with God. We are stuck in the flesh. We forget to live by faith and not by sight. We forget how we should live. Luke 4:4 says, "It is written, that man shall not live by bread alone, but by every word of God." We should read our Bibles and study the word.

We have the tools. In addition to the word of God, Ephesians 6: 13-17, tells us to put on the whole armor of God. This includes the belt of truth, the breastplate of righteousness, feet fitted with readiness, the shield of faith, the helmet of salvation, and the sword of the Spirit. With this armor, we will be able to stand our ground, and after we have done everything, we will still be able to stand.

Sentence two of the opening lines to Mission Impossible says, "As always, should you or any of your I.M. Force be caught or killed, the Secretary will disavow any knowledge of your actions. We will not get caught. We can succeed. God has gifted us, each of us, for such a time as this. Ephesians 6:19 says whenever we speak, words will be given to us so that we will fearlessly make known the mystery of the gospel. I am so glad that our heavenly father will not disavow us. The Bible says he will blot out our transgressions and remember them no more. He gives us new mercies every morning. And he calls us good and faithful servants.

Finally, sentence three of the opening lines to Mission Impossible says, "This tape will self-destruct in five seconds." I am so glad that God's word and promises will not self-destruct. If we do our part, the Bible says He has prepared a place for us and when he comes again, he will receive us unto himself (John 14:3). Thank God for his promise.

Prayer

Lord, thank you for equipping us to accept and complete any mission you send us. Thank you for informing us of our role and fortifying us with the tools we need to be successful. You are an awesome God who makes all things possible. Amen

Reflection

What are my key takeaways from this teaching?

Do I understand my role on God's team?

What do I need to be successful?

What are my next steps?

Things Old & New

There is a renewed fascination and appreciation of all things mid-century modern, retro, and old school. Vinyl records, functional furniture, natural hairstyles, and a return to good home training are gaining popularity and in some circles are in fashion again. However, there are some old things we need to toss out. Some old things we need to stop doing; some old habits we need to break; and some old attitudes we need to change. Some old ... you fill in the blank.

As Christians, when we give our lives to the Lord, we are transformed into new creatures (2 Corinthians 5:17) and we take off the old self and put on a new spirit (Colossians 3:9-11) as we rise to a new life in Christ (Romans 6: 3-4). Taking on a new life or embarking on a new beginning is sometimes scary, unpredictable, difficult, or confusing, yet it is always worthwhile. We can trust the Lord to walk with us during this transition. He renews us daily (2 Corinthians 4: 16-17) and gives us a new spirit (Ezekial 11:19 & 36:26).

To embrace new beginnings, first, let go of the past. Sometimes we get stuck in the cycle of should of, could of, would of ... you did, they did, I did. We can never move forward looking in the rearview mirror. That is why the front windshield is much bigger. We must forgive ourselves and others. God forgets our past (Hebrews 8:12) and does not consider former things. Instead, he does something new in our lives (Isaiah 43: 18-19). I thank God his mercies are new each morning (Lamentations 3:22-24). God can give us rest (Matthew 11:29) and peace (Philippians 4:7). He can provide us with directions (Proverbs 20 24) and give us grace (2 Corinthians 9:8). He can help us resist temptation (1 Corinthians 10:13); he can fulfill his every promise (Roman's 4:21). Stop looking back at them/it and start/keep looking forward at him. Let go of the past.

Second, know change can be good. It has been said that besides death and taxes, change is the only definite thing in life. The dictionary says change means to make something different or replace something with something else that is newer or better. When we give our lives to the Lord, we decide to make Jesus our choice. We trust him, depend on him, and follow him. We must commit to our different, new, and better life. Romans 6:4 says we can walk in the "newness of life" because the Lord makes all new. Acts 17:28 reminds us, "In him we live and move and have our being." Change can be good. When we need support, call on the Lord. Isaiah 55:6 encourages us to "seek the Lord while he may be found; call on him while he is near." The Lord is near to all who call on him (Psalms 145:18). This walk with Christ is wonderful; taste and see that the Lord is good (Psalm 34:8). Know change can be good.

Third, lean on gratitude. Letting go of the past and making a change are huge steps. It is often scary to travel this now unfamiliar and seemingly narrow path. We are not alone. The Lord goes before us, is with us, and will never leave us (Deuteronomy 31 8). Give thanks. He renews our strength daily (Isaiah 40:31). Give thanks. He will make our enemies our footstools (Luke 20:43). Give thanks. He is for us and none can be against us (Romans 8:31). Give thanks. He is a lamp unto our feet and a light to our path (Psalm 119:105). Give thanks. We are more than conquerors (Romans 8:37). Give thanks. Living a life filled with gratitude allows us to see the cup half full instead of half empty, we see abundance instead of lack, we are positive instead of negative, and we look at him and not at them. Lean on gratitude.

There is still a lot of good in some old things, old ways, and old ideals. This life with Christ is better than anything we have had before. How we move forward is based on how we choose to respond. The hymn says, "Yes, Lord, yes, to your will and way. Yes, Lord, yes, I will trust you and obey. When your Spirit speaks to me, with my whole heart I will agree. And my answer will be yes, Lord, yes!" With an open and grateful heart, say yes!

Prayer

Lord, I am ready for a new beginning. Come into my life, I am ready to say yes. Assist me to let go of the past, to see the good in change, and to be grateful for you. Amen.

Reflection

What are my key takeaways from this teaching?

What do I need to leave in the past?

What do I need to change?

What are my next steps?

Nuggets of Encouragement: Living Each Day with Grace & Love

Shout to the Lord

A couple of times a week, there is a 3:00 AM train that crosses the railroad track about a mile or so from my house. Sometimes I am awake when it barrels through; sometimes it awakens me. I often wonder what kind of train it is. Is it a freight train or a passenger train? How many cars is the engine pulling? How fast is it going? It is interesting how the sound, the rumble, and the clackety-clack of the wheels on the rails, waft through the air and make a big sound.

Several passages in the Bible attest to the power of sound. Genesis 3:8 is one of the first scriptures that talks about sound. The verse says, "They heard the sound of the Lord God walking in the garden in the cool of the day." It was audible, a big sound, Adam and Eve hid themselves. Has God ever walked in your life? Have you ever hidden from God?

God frequently walks through our lives. For some, his presence goes unnoticed. My grandma used to say, "Thank God for waking you up each day clothed in your right mind with the use and activity of your limbs. You did not have to wake up this morning and the bed you slept in could have been your cooling board." Amen. Take notice. For in "Him we live and have our being," (Acts 17:28). Sometimes God walks through, at other times he walks before us, behind us, or beside us. Many times, he carries us. God is always there for us.

When Ezekiel shared his vision of God's glory returning to the temple, he noted that God's "voice was like a noise of many waters," (Ezekiel 43:2). Job 37:2 says, "hear attentively the thunder of his [God's] voice, and the rumbling that comes from his mouth." John also talked about the voice of God. Revelations 14:2, says, "And I heard a voice from heaven as the voice of many waters, and as the voice of a great thunder." Have you ever heard the noise or thunder of God's voice? Did you hide from it or did you bask in the glory and awe of it?

There is never a need to hide from God. He is omnipresent. He sees all, knows all, and suffers all to be so. Jeremiah 23:24 says, "Can any hide himself in secret places that I shall not see him? saith the Lord. Do not I fill heaven and earth? saith the Lord." Psalm 139:12 adds that even in darkness, you cannot hide. For many of us, we have had times when our actions and decision-making have not been stellar. Frankly, we may have wanted to hide. Even in those times, God was always there for us.

There are other examples of the power of sound in the Bible. At Pentecost, a sound came from heaven. Acts 2:2 says it sounded like a "rushing mighty wind." When David fought against the Philistines, the Lord told him to wait to strike until he heard marching in the tops of the trees (2 Samuel 5:24). When Joshua and his army marched on Jericho, he was told to wait until he heard a long blast and then to have his army give a loud shout. The walls of the city fell (Joshua 6:5).

Has God ever told you to wait? Has he ever orchestrated a victory in your life? Did you use the sound of your voice, your hands, or your feet to give thanks? God is our number one cheerleader. He loved us so much that he gave his only begotten son so we would not perish and have everlasting life (John 3:16). He deserves our praise.

Psalm 47:1 tells us to clap our hands and shout to God with the voice of triumph. Psalm 100:1 encourages us to make a joyful noise unto the Lord. If we can hoot and holler at sporting events, concerts, and other venues, we can hoot and holler for the Lord. Remember, different kinds of praise may require us to make noise. For example, Shabach means to shout! Taquah means to clap your hands. Yadah means to extend your hands. Towdah means to lift your hands. Tehilah means to sing! Halal means to celebrate and Kara means to dance. "Come, let us sing for joy to the Lord; let us shout aloud to the Rock of our salvation," (Psalms 95:1). Give him praise.

Prayer

Lord, thank you for your being. Sometimes you come in a loud noise, a rumble, a rushing mighty wind, the voice of great thunder, the sound of many waters, or even in a still small voice. No matter the circumstance, you are always there for us. For this, I thank you, thank you, thank you. Amen

Reflection

What are my key takeaways from this teaching?

When was the last time God walked in your life? What was the result?

When was the last time you talked to God? What was the result?

What are my next steps?

Nuggets of Encouragement: Living Each Day with Grace & Love

A Sweet Aroma: The Nose Knows

When I was a kid, my dad would pile my mom, my siblings, and me into the Studebaker and go for a ride in the country. On almost every trip, an awful smell would waft through the windows. Dad would say, "Ooh, Ooh, I smell a pole cat." We would pinch our noses and fan the air. Momma would pass around a hankie she had sprinkled with White Shoulders. We would each take a whiff; like magic, the smell would dissipate. The nose knows.

The sense of smell is one of those things to which almost everyone can relate. Most know what it means to smell something fresh, faint, light, floral, rank, airy, musty, stale, or stinky. If our lives were defined by smell, would someone say, "Ooh, I smell a pleasing aroma" or "Ooh, Ooh, I smell a pole cat?" The nose knows.

The Bible talks to us about pleasing aromas. 2 Corinthians 2:15 says, "For we are unto God a sweet savor of Christ." Paul says that our lives before God are "An odor of a sweet smell, a sacrifice acceptable, well pleasing to God," (Philippians 4:18). In Ezekiel 20:41, God says, "I will accept you as fragrant incense."

Amen, what a joy to be accepted as a sweet aroma to the Lord. The nose knows.

Consider this acronym for aroma:

A*greeable* – sweet disposition!

Reverence – submissive and humble spirit!

Obedience – saying "Yes, Lord"!

Music – singing praises!

Agape – sacrificial, unconditional love for both other Christians and the lost!

The nose knows. What do we smell like? Many of us have had some pole cats in our lives. For some people, the smell has long gone; for some, it still stinks. Being in the presence of God regularly, reading, and meditating on the word should help Him to rub off on us. Others should see Him in us and smell the sweet aroma of Him on us. The nose knows.

Remember the wonder-working power of the blood of the Lamb. When we met the Lord, He transformed us into new creatures. He washed us, turned us around, and set our feet on solid ground. Ephesians 5:2 tells us to "Walk in the way of love, just as Christ loved us and gave himself up for us as a fragrant offering and sacrifice to God."

Prayer

Lord, through your mercy and your grace, may the pole cats be removed from our lives. "May my prayer come to You like the sweet smell of incense," (Psalm 141:2). May we always be a sweet aroma: the nose knows. Amen.

Reflection

What are my key takeaways from this teaching?

Do I like the way I smell? Why? Why not?

Are there pole cats in my life? So what?

What are my next steps?

What's Love Got to Do with it?

Love is something that everyone is seeking. We look for it in people and things. Statistics indicate that 2023 spending for Valentine's Day was $26 billion. That is a lot of money. But what does love have to do with it? Mother's Day is another big spender. It is estimated that Americans spent over $31 billion on Mother's Day and $20 billion on Father's Day in 2022. Again, that is a lot of money. But what does love have to do with it?

I am like most folks; I like getting presents. I also like giving. Question, do we need a holiday to express our love for one another? Do we need to spend billions? I say no. Love does not cost a thing. It should be ever-present in our lives. Love is the perfect gift, the ultimate gift. God so loved the world, that he gave his only begotten son. It did not cost us a thing! Because of that love, unconditional, everlasting, and steadfast, we can reap the benefits of God's unfailing love. In Psalm 103 David outlines the benefits of God's love. Briefly, He forgives all our iniquities, He heals our diseases, He redeems our lives from the pit, He crowns us with steadfast love and mercy, and He satisfies us with good. Amen, now that is love! God is love.

What the Lord asks us in return is simple. He told us to love our neighbors as ourselves as it was the second greatest of the commandments. The Bible calls for us to show sincere love, to let everything we do be done in love, and to clothe ourselves in love. We are in a time when there is so much and so many we might find unlovable. Yes, we can; we can show love. 1 Corinthians 13:4-8 says "Love is patient and kind. Love is not jealous or boastful or proud or rude. Love does not demand its way. Love is not irritable, and it keeps no record of when it has been wronged. It is never glad about injustice but rejoices whenever the truth wins out. Love never gives up, never loses faith, is always hopeful, and endures through every circumstance. Love will last forever."

We are all imperfect human beings. Sometimes we walk by sight and not by faith. Sometimes we have to dig deep to show love. At those times, let us look to the hills whence comes our help. Let us open our hearts and do it. Love is not in our wallets but in our hearts. Hebrews 6:19 reminds us that, "love anchors the soul."

Let us be like the little train and stop saying I think I can and start saying I know I can. When the tide is rough, when all else fails, and when nothing else can help, love can lift you and me. And it does not cost a thing!

Prayer

Father, the lifter of my head, search me and give me a clean heart. I desire to have a love that endures all and never gives up. With you, I know this is possible and I count it done. Amen

Reflection

What are my key takeaways from this teaching?

Nuggets of Encouragement: Living Each Day with Grace & Love

To whom do I need to extend 1 Corinthians 13 kind of love?

What are some ways I can extend love to others?

What are my next steps?

Addition or Submission

I used to be a math teacher. From a math perspective, addition is a wonderful thing. It is the process of adding one thing to another and ending up with more. More, that is a big word. There was no way anyone could tell me that there was anything better than addition other than multiplication. You also get more when you perform that mathematical operation. There is that word again—more. Sounds good, right? Hmm...

Consider that there is something better than addition that equals more gained by multiplication. That would be submission. I recently watched the movie *A Matter of Faith*. One of the characters asked an intriguing question of another. He asked, "Have you added Jesus to your life or have you submitted to Him?" Wow! Think about addition or submission.

The dictionary says submission is the action or fact of accepting or yielding to a superior force. What does this have to do with more? Submitting your life to the Lord equals more of everything. James 4:7 tells us to submit ourselves to God. 1 Peter 2:13 says to "submit yourselves for the Lord's sake." Submission to God means that we obey Him, we listen to Him, we lean on Him, we put our faith in Him, and we follow Him.

When we submit to the Lord, our lives equal more. Matthew 6:33 tells us, "But seek first His kingdom and His righteousness and all these things will be added to you." Should we worship God just to get more? No, God does not need us. Acts 17: 24-25 tells us, "The God who made the world and everything in it is the Lord of heaven and earth and does not live in temples built by human hands. And He is not served by human hands, as if He needed anything. Rather, He gives everyone life and breath and everything else." God owns everything (Genesis 14:19, Psalm 24:1, Job 41:11, Psalm 50:10-12). He has no needs and owes nothing to anyone.

God does not need us, but we desperately need Him. We need His compassion, His love, His mercy, His forgiveness, His protection, His healing, His direction, His grace, and His peace. This is the more we need and may obtain through submission. God will give us the desires of our hearts (Psalm 37:4). He freely gives all things to us (Romans 8:32).

God does not ask us to add or multiply, instead He requires us, "to act justly, and to love mercy and to walk humbly with your God," (Micah 6:8). Walking in submission to the Lord is more, exceedingly, abundantly more than anyone could ask or think.

Prayer

Heavenly Father, I want to submit my life, my will, and my way to you. Lead me, guide me, and show me the way to salvation. Amen.

Reflection

What are my key takeaways from this teaching?

Have I been adding God to my life?

What do I need to do to fully submit to God?

What are my next steps?

What do I do with the Crumbs?

The dictionary says a crumb is a small piece broken from a baked item, such as a cookie, cake, or bread. It is also a small fragment, scrap, or portion. Have you ever thought about the value of a crumb? I once saw a colony of ants at work, each carrying a crumb back to their nest. Amazingly, they can carry up to 50 times their weight. A crumb can be seen as something good or bad, as a positive or a negative thing. It depends on if we see the container as half full or half empty. It depends; do we see abundance or lack? Like an ant, I see abundance.

Question: What can you do with crumbs? Have you ever eaten something so good that you moistened your fingertips to pick up every crumb? I have. Have you ever used bread crumbs to enhance a recipe? I have. Crumbs can be used to make a good pan of dressing, a sweet bread pudding, a juicy meatloaf, a savory casserole, homemade crotons, or you can use them to sop up some gravy. Yum, Yum!

My momma told me that when she was growing up, they were so poor that her mother would save the bread crumbs and crusts, and once a week she would put them in a bowl and pour buttermilk over them. That would be their dinner. Question: Abundance or lack? In Luke 16:21 we read that Lazarus was longing to be fed with the crumbs which were falling from the rich man's table. Question: Abundance or lack? The Bible says when Lazarus died, "the angels carried him to Abraham's side." In Matthew 15:27, we read about the Canaanite woman who said, "The dogs eat of the crumbs which fall from their masters' table." Question: Abundance or lack? The Bible says that because the woman had great faith, the Lord granted her request, and "her daughter was healed at that moment."

The Bible is filled with stories of abundance—of the Lord taking the crumbs and doing a lot with them. You know the story of Elijah's encounter with the widow who had a handful of flour in a jar and a little oil in a jug. After she obediently used her crumbs—the last that she had—to make a cake for Elijah, her jar and jug were miraculously filled. You also know how Jesus fed five thousand with two fish and five loaves of bread. And, when the meal was finished, the Bible says, "The disciples picked up twelve basketfuls of broken pieces that were left over." They collected all the crumbs. In each story, a little was turned into a lot.

Whether we have a few crumbs or a lot of crumbs, we must keep our eyes on Jesus. We cannot let the stress and the noise of life cloud our vision or hinder us from hearing God's still, small voice. Proverbs 17:1 says, "Better a dry crust with peace than a house full of feasting, with strife."

Can we trust our awesome God to do a lot with the little crumbs we have? I say yes, Lord, yes.

2 Corinthians 9:8 says, "God can bless you abundantly, so that in all things at all times, having all that you need, you will abound in every good work."

Prayer

God, you are the God of abundance. You are the giver and multiplier of our crumbs. I love you and thank you for all you give to me. I choose to see abundance and not lack. I know through you all my needs will be met. Amen.

Reflection

What are my key takeaways from this teaching?

What are the areas of lack in my life?

What are the areas of abundance in my life?

What are my next steps?

M.O.N.E.Y.

By the title you probably think this piece is about dead presidents, greenbacks, cash, currency, bread, bucks, loot, legal tender, dough, wads, Benjamin's, moola, lucre, wampum, folding stuff, or Gs. Nope! I am not going to get into your pocketbook or your wallet. But I am going to talk about M.O.N.E.Y.

M is for mercy. God's mercy is great above the heavens (Psalm 108:4). Hebrew 4:16 says, "Let us then approach God's throne of grace with confidence, so that we may receive mercy and find grace to help us in our time of need." If it were not for God's mercy and grace, I do not know where I would be. He has been a healer, a confidant, a companion, and a comforter. He has been a way out of no way, a protector, a shield, a strong tower, a teacher, a provider, and so much more. If I spoke for an hour, I could not tell it all. He has been that much to me. Even more for me to show mercy and grace in my interactions with my fellow man.

O is for the opportunity to serve. 2 Corinthians 9:12 speaks of service. It says, "This service that you perform is not only supplying the needs of the Lord's people but is also overflowing in many expressions of thanks to God." Ephesians 4:12 says that service builds up the "body of Christ." And James 2:26 is clear that "faith without works is dead." God expects us to use our time to provide service to others. If Jesus served, why cannot we?

N means never forget that our Christian walk is full of trials, tests, and battles. The Lord never promised us an easy walk. Look at what he endured. 1 Peter 4:12 tells us not to think it strange when things come to test us. James 1:2 tells us to count it all joy when we meet trials of various kinds. And, Joshua 1:9 says, "Be strong and courageous. Do not be frightened, and do not be dismayed, for the Lord your God is with you wherever you go." Let me encourage you to remember why you have chosen this walk. Suit up! Put your war clothes on and trust in God. The rewards are worth it all. The song says,

E is for ears and eyes. Proverbs 20:12 says, "Ears that hear and eyes that see. The Lord made them both." We should use our ears to hear the Lord's voice and to understand what he is saying to us. The Lord speaks in a still, small voice. It is up to us to close out the noise of our overly busy lives so we can hear him. Paul was on the road to Damascus when he heard the voice of God (Acts 9: 1-19). Moses, Isaiah, Samuel, John, Cornelius, Ezekial, Peter, and Elijah all heard and headed the voice of God. The Lord said in John 10:27, "My sheep hear My voice, and I know them, and they follow Me." The Lord has a job for us and needs us to hear him and be ready to act. It has been said that the eyes are the windows to the souls. What do you see from your windows? I see that God is all around us and is still in the healing, blessing, and miracle-working business. Sometimes the cares of the world shield our eyes and keep us from seeing the glory of God. Psalm 119:18 says, "Open my eyes, that I may behold wonderful things from Your law." Ephesians 1:18 says, "I pray that the eyes of your heart may be enlightened, so that you will know what is the hope to which he has called you."

Finally, Y is for Yes, Lord. Saying yes to the Lord should be, but it is not always an easy task. We are often overwhelmed or doubtful about our ability to complete the job or mission that God has given us. Whenever God gives us a task, he has already gone before us to prepare the way. God asks extraordinary things from ordinary people. Remember, Mary said yes to the conception of our Savior. Noah said yes to building the ark. Moses said yes as he stood before the burning bush. David said yes when he took the challenge to fight Goliath. Esther said yes when she went to see the king. 1 Corinthians 15:58 says, "Always give yourselves fully to the work of the Lord because you know that your labor is not in vain."

Prayer

We each have money we can use and the opportunity to serve is forever present. Help us never forget the challenges and rewards of our Christian walk. We each have ears to hear and eyes to see. Let us use all that we have to say yes to you. Amen.

Reflection

What are my key takeaways from this teaching?

M.O.N.E.Y.—to which area do I need to give more attention?

Have I said yes to God? Why/why not?

What are my next steps?

Recap & Apply

What have I learned about God's love?

How will I apply this learning to my life?

What have I learned about God's grace?

How will I apply this learning to my life?

About the Author

A church liturgist, Sunday School and Vacation Bible School teacher, and Bible study instructor are a few of the roles Dr. Rebekah McCloud has held. In 2004, she added church historian to the list when awarded the Rhea Marsh and Dorothy Smith Winter Park History Research Grant sponsored by the Winter Park Public Library and Rollins College. Her project and resulting book, Across the Tracks: A Collective History of Black Churches of Winter Park (FL), chronicles the history of the six oldest Black churches in Winter Park. Her follow-up to the project, sponsored by the City of Winter Park, was a book, Sacred Places, Sacred History: Black Churches of Winter Park. It chronicled the beginnings of Winter Park and Hannibal Square, the development of the twelve churches, and several of the citizens who contributed to the development of the West Side. She has continued that work over the years by photographing and collecting information on more than 50 historic black churches in Florida, Georgia, and Alabama. Currently, Dr. McCloud is working on a series of Christian journals. A retired educator who most recently served as the Executive Director of TRIO Programs at the University of Central Florida

(UCF), Dr. McCloud is a former school principal and an awarded classroom teacher who has taught undergraduate and graduate courses at several institutions. An author and award-winning journalist, she served on the editorial review board for six national peer-reviewed journals. She has shared her wisdom through over 200 workshops at local, state, regional, and national conferences. A versatile educator, in addition to being a certified Florida teacher and school administrator, she is a Certified Life Coach, a Certified Practitioner in Financial Capability, and a certified Financial Education Instructor. Dr. McCloud holds an Ed.D. in Curriculum & Instruction, a M.S in Business (Managerial Leadership), a M.Ed. in Education (Educational Leadership), a B.A. in Communications, and a Graduate Certificate in Career & Technical Education.

Further Study

For Further Study, see the three journals in the series:
- Journal 1— Nuggets of Encouragement: Living Each Day with Grace & Love
- Journal 2— Nuggets of Encouragement: Receiving God's Blessing Through Our Christian Walk
- Journal 3—Nuggets of Encouragement: Learning to Trust and Have Faith in God

Praise for *Nuggets of Encouragement*
What Readers Are Saying

Nuggets of Encouragement is a devotional that points the reader straight to the word of God. Each nugget contains personal stories and anecdotes that connect everyday life to scripture. I am personally enriched by the verses that are carefully selected in each writing. This devotional is an excellent resource for both personal reflection and group study. You will be blessed to grow and learn from the biblical applications in each nugget!
—Hiroko Vargas

Dr. Rebekah's Nuggets of Encouragement is full of wisdom and insight! This transformative book is your roadmap to life and life choices, dedicated to providing valuable guidance, inspiration, and practical advice to viewers. By serving as a guidepost, Nuggets of Encouragement offers readers a roadmap to navigate life's challenges and make informed decisions. The thought-provoking content sparks introspection, encourages personal growth, and empowers individuals to make conscious choices that align with their values and aspirations. Dr. McCloud provides engaging segments that present a collection of powerful insights and lessons from various sources, including ancient wisdom, spiritual teachings, philosophical concepts, and personal experiences. Whether you are seeking clarity, motivation, or a deeper understanding of yourself and the world around you, this book offers a treasure trove of wisdom to enrich and elevate your life journey. Explore the depths of wisdom and insight to help you on your path to personal growth and fulfillment.

—Dr. Tuyna Griffin, Founder & CEO, Black Women's Voices

Gifted, called, and anointed for a time such as this, Dr. Rebekah McCloud is walking in her divine calling. She is doing what she does best. I have enjoyed reading Dr. Rebekah McCloud's nuggets. She is very knowledgeable of the word of God and she always incorporates her life experiences into her nuggets. So glad to see her walking in her calling. She is a very kind person and she represents the Father well. I look forward to hearing future words of wisdom from Dr. Rebekah. Keep those nuggets coming!

—Patricia Eason, CEO, Angels Without Wings

Thank you, Dr. Rebekah, for this thought-provoking, inspirational, encouraging, and uplifting journal of daily nuggets to help get you through the day and beyond. I love your candid personal stories and how refreshing you have a way with words. I pray that this journal will bless all who read it. May God bless you and keep you always and that you remain in the center of His will.

—Patricia Washington, Pastor, Grace for Living Ministries

I do not believe anyone is more excited about this journal than I am. I have been the recipient of Dr. McCloud's wisdom, spirituality, humor, and amazing storytelling since 2019. Dr. McCloud's devotions have encouraged, inspired, and challenged me in my daily walk with Christ. I have been asking her for years to put her weekly nuggets into a book. I plan to be the first to order this journal, and I pray that if you are reading this you will join me in supporting this phenomenal woman and the gift that God has placed inside of her.

—Dr. Coretta Cotton

www.ingramcontent.com/pod-product-compliance
Lightning Source LLC
Chambersburg PA
CBHW031423290426
44110CB00011B/496